Golden Tales of the Thracians
Treasure, Myth, and Legend

Table of Contents

1. Introduction 1
2. The Dawn of Thracian Civilization 2
   - 2.1. The Earliest Evidence 2
   - 2.2. The Emergence of Tribal Structures 3
   - 2.3. The Golden Age of Metallurgy 3
   - 2.4. Expansion and Interaction 4
   - 2.5. Conclusion 4
3. Legends Interwoven in Thracian History 5
   - 3.1. The Tale of Orpheus and Eurydice 5
   - 3.2. The God Dionysus: A Dual Legacy 6
   - 3.3. Rhesus of Thrace: The Hero of the Trojan War 6
   - 3.4. Sacred Tattoos: Mythology Inked onto Skin 7
   - 3.5. Legacy Through Metal: Thracian Treasures 7
4. Unveiling the Golden Treasures 9
   - 4.1. The Thracian's Gold 9
   - 4.2. The Oeuvre of Thracian Goldsmiths 10
   - 4.3. The Narratives within the Gold 11
   - 4.4. The Legacy of Thracian Gold Treasures 11
5. Mythology and Thracian Gods 13
   - 5.1. The Pantheon of Thracian Deities 13
   - 5.2. The Influence of Greek Mythology 14
   - 5.3. Thracian Rituals and Customs 14
   - 5.4. Thracian Deities' Depictions in Art 15
   - 5.5. Reflection on the Thracian Belief System 16
6. Sacred Rituals and Their Meaning 17
   - 6.1. The Horse Sacrifice 17
   - 6.2. Funerary Rituals 17
   - 6.3. Ritual of Tattooing 18

- 6.4. Feast of Dionysus 18
- 6.5. Oracle Rituals 19
- 7. Kings and Warriors: The Pillars of Thracian Society 20
  - 7.1. Thracian Kings: A Confluence of Power and Wisdom 20
  - 7.2. The Warrior Code: Unleashing the Strength of the Thracians 21
  - 7.3. Warrior Women of Thrace 21
  - 7.4. Kings and Warriors: The Dynamic Duo 22
  - 7.5. A Legacy of Valor 22
- 8. Mystery of the Thracian Tombs 23
  - 8.1. The Discovery 23
  - 8.2. Description of a Typical Thracian Tomb 24
  - 8.3. Artefacts Uncovered 24
  - 8.4. The Enigma of the Tombs 25
- 9. Artistic Brilliance: Thracian Goldsmiths 26
  - 9.1. The Pinnacle of Mastery 26
  - 9.2. Golden Artifacts of Ancient Thracians 26
  - 9.3. Techniques of the Golden Age 27
  - 9.4. Ritualistic Affluence 28
  - 9.5. The Legacy of the Golden Age 28
- 10. Influence on Neighboring Civilizations 30
  - 10.1. Artistic Influence 30
  - 10.2. Influence on Military 31
  - 10.3. The Impact on Religion and Mythology 31
  - 10.4. Social and Political Influence 32
  - 10.5. Conclusion 32
- 11. Legacy of the Thracians: A Retrospective Glance 33
  - 11.1. The Origins of the Thracian Civilization 33
  - 11.2. The Emanation of Thracian Art and Metalwork 33
  - 11.3. Warriors of Thracia 34

11.4. Interfaces of Influence: Greek, Persian, and Roman 34
11.5. Linguistic Legacy 35
11.6. Conclusion: The Echoes of Thracian Legacy 35

Chapter 1. Introduction

Unearth the radiant past of the Thracians as never before with our Special Report: "Golden Tales of the Thracians: Treasure, Myth, and Legend". Journey back in time and be enthralled by the magnificent treasures, unparalleled myths, and fascinating legends that shaped one of Europe's earliest and most mysterious civilizations. This report, brimming with compelling narratives, breathtaking imagery, and enriched by expert insights is not only an immersive read but also a visual spectacle to behold. A reality beyond your everyday lives, a historical saga waiting to transform your perspective, this is an adventurous investment you won't regret. The sparkling allure of ancient Thracian gold is calling – dare to dive into the depths of the unknown and discover a world untouched by time!

Chapter 2. The Dawn of Thracian Civilization

In the uncharted corridors of Europe's past, a civilization emerged, consistent powerful, and inherently enduring. The Thracians, an ancient and enigmatic society, formed settlements around 4000 B.C., in present-day Southeast Europe. Their land, now divided into modern territories like Bulgaria, Greece, and Turkey, was then a realm of dynamic cultures blending, culminating in a sophisticated civilization that left an indelible imprint upon the annals of history. This chapter embarks on a meticulous exploration of the Thracian civilization's dawn.

2.1. The Earliest Evidence

Archeologists have long been fascinated with delineating the roots of Thracian civilization. The earliest pieces of evidence, mainly drawn from burial mounds and archaeological sites throughout the Thracian heartland, sweepingly signify a cultured society. Burial gifts found in these mounds range from beautifully wrought golden treasures and intricately designed clay vessels to weapons forged with skilled craftsmanship and precious jewels.

Through the meticulous study of clay pot designs and dimensions, archaeologists have established the Thracians' extraordinary artistic sensibility and their predomination toward symbolic narrative depictions. Material culture analysis indicates that these early Thracian communities were agrarian in nature, underpinned by animal husbandry, farming, and rudimentary metallurgy. Unlike their Aegean neighbors, the Thracians did not develop palatial states, instead opting for decentralized, tribal societies.

2.2. The Emergence of Tribal Structures

The evolution of Thracian society bore semblance to other ancient civilization structures, marked by the emergence of tribal hierarchies. Disparate, yet close-knit farming and herding communities began to congeal under the authority of tribal leaders, these were typically individuals of valor or of wisdom, or both. Evidently, the military might played a defining role in these societies, reflected through higher-status burials infused with weapons and warrior symbolism.

Moreover, mythological depictions on artifacts hint at the rise of a complex pantheon, governed by a horse-riding deity. The horse, a symbol of power, freedom, and military prowess, was a central aspect of Thracian society, as were splendid feasts and music, often illustrated on pottery and infused into metalwork.

2.3. The Golden Age of Metallurgy

As time drew on, Thracian society rode the crest of early Bronze Age advancements. Enriched by lands abundant with minerals, Thracian craftsmen honed their skills, moving from simple copper and tin alloy metals to intricate gold and silver work, ushering in a golden age of metallurgy.

Artifacts unearthed from this period clearly demonstrate the Thracian's extraordinary mastery over metal, forming not just tools and weapons, but also intricate trinkets, jewelry, and adornments. Harnessing the fundamental essence of gold and other metals, their work represented an intriguing blend of practicality and aesthetics, with motifs narrating tales of godly feats, battles, and daily life activities.

2.4. Expansion and Interaction

Due to their strategic geographical position, the Thracians were participants and observers in the interplay of cultures. The civilization's expansion is marked by artifacts unearthed miles from their homeland, testifying to their trading prowess. Evidence of Mycenaean and Aegean influence indicates that the Thracians were partaking in Mediterranean trade networks, exchanging raw materials and artisan crafts.

Scholars have confirmed the presence of Thracian wares in Anatolia, likening to the cultural exchange between the Thracians and the burgeoning empires of the East. Concurrently, elements of Thracian style appeared as far as Italy, signifying their widespread reach and influence.

2.5. Conclusion

Thus began the remarkable journey of an ancient civilization, interwoven with the unraveling of Europe's tapestry. The Thracians' dawn encapsulated the establishment of an agricultural society, the evolution of tribal structures, the pioneering expeditions into metallurgy, and the dynamic cultural exchanges with neighboring civilizations. Across the endless tumults of time, the echoes of Thracian civilization continue to resonate, rendering their history an enriching narrative of human resilience and ingenuity.

Chapter 3. Legends Interwoven in Thracian History

Nestled deep in the annals of Europe's primal lineage draws a vibrant yet complex tapestry - the Thracians. A civilization sinewy interlaced with myth and legend, where truth is seasoned with fantasy, and reality is often a dream spun on the loom of imagination.

3.1. The Tale of Orpheus and Eurydice

Prominent in Thracian mythology, Orpheus, the master lyre player, is a figure of considerable consequence. Born to the Muse Calliope, Orpheus was attributed to the region of Rhodope in Thracia. His legendary melodic prowess, said to move even the most inert objects, won him the admiration of gods and men.

Orpheus' legend finds its tragic arc in his love for Eurydice. During the couple's celebratory revelries upon their marriage, Eurydice was killed by a snake bite. Heartbroken, Orpheus dared to descend into the underworld, transfixing the guardians with his mournful melodies to an extent that Hades himself, the lord of the Underworld, granted him Eurydice's return. However, the condition was that he must not look back at her until they both reached daylight. In his anxiety, Orpheus defied the decree and glanced at Eurydice, who was then pulled back to the underworld forever.

3.2. The God Dionysus: A Dual Legacy

Dionysus, the divine patron of wine and ecstasy, also played a crucial role in Thracian lore. His dual Thracian-Greek heritage combines the elements of extreme pleasure and primal terror, representing the fine line between joy and horror.

Foremost narratives represent Dionysus as the son of Zeus and the Thracian princess Semele. Hera, in her jealousy, deceived Semele into demanding Zeus reveal himself in all his divine glory, leading to her instantaneous incineration. Zeus then rescued the unborn Dionysus and sewed him into his thigh until he was ready to be born.

Dionysus' devotees, the Maenads, divulged their uninhibited spirit during his wild rites. The Bacchanalia, as the Dionysian festivals were known, were renowned for their ecstatic dancing and indulgence in wine - a perfect manifestation of Dionysian influence.

3.3. Rhesus of Thrace: The Hero of the Trojan War

Rhesus, another significant character hailing from Thrace, was a mythological king, who met his fate fighting against the Greeks in the Trojan War. The legend of Rhesus is most known from Euripides' play "Rhesus," which portrays the Thracian king's arrival on the battlefield and his subsequent death in a single night.

The Homeric traditions narrate how Dolon, a Trojan, promised to sneak the Greeks' plans in return for Achilles' horses. However, on being captured by Odysseus and Diomedes, Dolon disclosed Rhesus' arrival. This led to the ambush and killing of Rhesus and his men while they were asleep, thus depriving the Trojans of his help.

3.4. Sacred Tattoos: Mythology Inked onto Skin

The Thracians were known for their penchant for tattoos, considered symbolically significant. Thracian tattoos were not mere adornments but sacred markers linking them to their favored deity. Herodotus mentions the Thracian tribes of the Getae, believed to be immortal, marked their bodies with elaborate tattoos to establish divine association.

This practice was mirrored by the Oracle of Dionysius, found in the Rhodope Mountains, who was depicted with tattoos of ivy leaves, symbolizing her dedication to the god. Thus, in the collective mythological conscience, the Thracians were seen as vying for a form of eternal life - either through marking their bodies with tattoos in the present life or seeking immortality in the afterlife.

3.5. Legacy Through Metal: Thracian Treasures

The lore of the Thracians has not only survived through verbal continuation but also has been recorded in their magnificent treasures. Thracian rulers immortalized their beliefs, myths, and victories in funerary objects left in burial mounds, leading to some of the most impressive archaeological discoveries of gold and silver artifacts.

One of the iconic representations is the Panagyurishte Gold Treasure found in Central Bulgaria, involving a collection of intricately designed golden vessels depicting scenes from Thracian mythology. Predominant among them are the amphora and phiales displaying scenes of Dionysian rites, emphasizing the high regard held for the god.

The Thracians' history offers an intoxicating concoction of fantasy, myth, and legend blending with tangible history. This intertwining of lore and reality does not merely add dimension and volume to their existence but also paints a multi-dimensional picture of a civilization whose roots remain as bewildering as they are fascinating. It is this realm of the mystical and the tangible that reveals the Thracian civilization's layered and rhythmic dance with time, creating a legacy that continues to mystify and enthrall.

Chapter 4. Unveiling the Golden Treasures

The Thracian civilization was rich in abundant gold resources, unrivaled metalworking skills, and a deep-rooted mythological belief system, each of which intertwined with the others, blessing them with an enormous treasury brimming full of golden artefacts. These treasures didn't simply shine with the vibrancy of their material but also illuminated the rich culture, stories, and lives of the Thracians that crafted them.

4.1. The Thracian's Gold

Gold held a marked prominence within the Thracian culture. Sources suggest that the Thracians were among the earliest civilizations to mine and work with gold. The region – now encompassing parts of modern-day Bulgaria, Greece, and Turkey – was richly endowed with gold deposits. These precious resources, along with the Thracians' innate knack for metalworking, birthed an era of prosperity and affluence.

Corroborating archaeological finds indicate that Thracian gold mining and refining operations were widespread and sophisticated, with numerous sites dotted around what are now the Rhodope Mountains in Bulgaria. Meanwhile, Thasos – a gold-rich island located not far from the Thracian mainland – bustled with Thracian mining activities, where the rivers reportedly contained particles of gold within their sands.

The Thracians' obsession with gold wasn't simply a fascination for its mere physical value. Gold was ingrained within their belief system and cultural practices. It was a sacred substance symbolizing the sun and its life-giving properties. As a vibrant symbol of power, divine favor, and immortality, gold was often incorporated into religious rites and elite graves, maintaining an enduring presence across the span of Thracian civilization.

4.2. The Oeuvre of Thracian Goldsmiths

The Thracians' deftness in incorporating gold in their lives is not spoken more profoundly than through the work of their skilled goldsmiths. Their craftsmanship, evident in the intricate designs and minute detailing of the artifacts, pervades the world of archaeology and antiquity until today.

Golden artifacts stretching thousands of years showcase an evolutionary history of Thracian metalworking. Incised and embossed plates, elegantly twisted and coiled jewelry, and exquisitely formed figurines mirror the nuanced expertise attained by the Thracian goldsmiths over the course of centuries.

Especially notable are their artfully designed rhytons – drinking vessels often taking the shape of animals or mythical beings – exemplifying delicate detailing, imaginative depiction, and masterful manipulation of gold. Similarly, golden jewelry often bestowed upon Thracian nobles and warriors – including necklaces, bracelets, pendants, and diadems – bear traces of the Thracians' detailed understanding of the malleability and endurance of gold.

To capture the nuances of life, the Thracians also incorporated techniques such as filigree and granulation to their goldworking practices. Granulation, using tiny globules of gold, helped reproduce intricate decorative patterns while filigree, utilizing fine, twisted threads of gold, offered a peculiar charm to the pieces.

4.3. The Narratives within the Gold

Imbued within the golden pieces were not just the aesthetic senses of the Thracian goldsmiths but also an intricate pattern of symbolic and narrative motifs. Heroes, gods, and mythical creatures often came to life in these masterpieces, embodying the Thracians' rich mythical and religious beliefs.

Among the most iconic of these symbols was the Thracian horseman – a divine entity believed to be a fusion of a local hero and the Greek god Hermes. Riding a horse, often accompanied by a dog following behind, the figure was a common motif among Thracian artifacts. Notably, the Rogozen Treasure – the largest Thracian treasure to have been discovered to date – pertinently features this motif across many of its pieces, casting insights into the religious life and afterlife beliefs of the Thracians.

Furthermore, mythic creatures and beasts also adorned the Thracian gold, serving both as protective and destructive forces. Griffins, sphinxes, lions, and serpents wove tales of valor, strength, and warning, often tying back to the central narrative of the piece.

4.4. The Legacy of Thracian Gold Treasures

The treasures left behind by the Thracians are today renowned worldwide, primarily due to their immense historical, artistic, and cultural value. Celebrated collections include the Panagyurishte Treasure, the Valchitran Treasure, and the aforementioned Rogozen Treasure. Each discovery exhumes stories from a bygone era, tales of the magnificent, golden past of the Thracians.

Just as the Thracians transformed gold, giving it new form and meaning, the study and preservation of these golden treasures today continue to shape our understanding of the Thracians. Unveiling these golden artifacts is like peeling away the layers of history, revealing the intricate tales of the Thracians' golden era.

In its entirety, the Thracian gold offers us a chance to delve deep into their cultural psyche. It is to step into a world glittering with stories and myths, fueled by imagination, and perfected by centuries of craftsmanship. And as we continue to uncover these treasures from the soil, with each artifact unearthed, we continue to unravel the golden tales of the Thracians, this fascinating civilization of the ancient past that still echoes through time.

Chapter 5. Mythology and Thracian Gods

The rich and vibrant tapestry of Thracian mythology is as intricate and complex as the culture it originated from. It is replete with intriguing gods and mythical beings, each with its unique narrative and influence on Thracian society. Shaped by a colorful mix of indigenous and borrowed beliefs, Thracian mythology provides a fascinating window into the Thracians' perspectives on life, death, nature, and the divine.

5.1. The Pantheon of Thracian Deities

Like many ancient civilizations, the Thracians worshipped a milieu of gods, each serving an individual function and filling a particular need of society. A snapshot of this divine assembly illustrates the gradation of life, nature, and magic, as seen through the Thracians' eyes.

The incomparable Zalmoxis is considered the most formidable god in the Thracian pantheon. He is credited as the god of life and death, an undertaking that granted him the title of "the most powerful." Zalmoxis was believed to reside in a cave in the wilderness, maintaining mysterious contact with his worshippers through enigmatic rituals. These rituals often involved the sacrifice of a messenger, adorned with numerous gifts aimed to secure Zalmoxis's favor.

Heros, another significant deity, was the horseman god of fertility and warfare. He was widely illustrated riding a horse, an iconic symbol of war and power. The Thracians saw Heros as a divine protector and invoked his blessing before going into battle.

The Thracian goddess Bendis was the embodiment of the moon, hunting, and wisdom. She was a favorite among the everyday populace due to her association with the critical sustenance activities of hunting and gathering.

Equally important was Sabazios, the enigmatic Thracian-Phrygian deity (who was later adopted by the Greeks and Romans) associated with sky, nature and, more specifically, oak trees. Intriguingly, he was often represented as a horseman, echoing the god Heros.

5.2. The Influence of Greek Mythology

Thracian mythology was not formed in a cultural vacuum. It absorbed elements from neighboring civilizations, especially that of the Greeks. From the 5th century BC onwards, direct contacts between the Thracians and Greeks increased, leading to mutual influence on religion, art, and culture. This amalgamation is most apparent in the mounting association of Thracian deities with those of the Greek pantheon.

Zalmoxis, for instance, was often linked with the Greek Great God, Dionysus, merging the former's life-death dynamism with Dionysus's ecstatic rituals. Similarly, the Thracian horseman god, Heros, was often equated to the Greek god Apollo, while Bendis acquired Athena's warrior wisdom.

5.3. Thracian Rituals and Customs

Thracian religious rituals were famously extravagant, engrossing, and steeped in mystery. The most reputable among these were the rituals associated with Zalmoxis. To communicate with their chief deity, worshippers diligently chose an envoy to bear their prayers and wishes. In an eerie ceremony, this messenger was then thrust on a spear or an arrow — a ritualistic sacrifice symbolizing his journey towards Zalmoxis. This openly sacrificial aspect distinguished the Zalmoxis cult from other contemporary religious practices.

Equally fascinating were the festivities associated with the cult of Dionysus-Zalmoxis. These were fervent rituals, drowned in wine, dance, and music, mirroring the very spirit of Dionysus.

5.4. Thracian Deities' Depictions in Art

Thracian mythology did not exist merely in an oral or written vacuum. It vividly permeated the material culture seen in various forms of art, sculptural depositions, and sumptuous grave goods. The Thracian deity art ranged from the grandeur of massive temple sculptures to the finesse of intricately carved golden treasures.

One of the most remarkable depictions of Thracian deities shines through in the Panagyurishte Treasure. This extraordinary gold artifact boasted proudly of Thracian craftsmanship and religious sentiments. Decorated with scenes embodying Dionysus-Zalmoxis, the Panagyurishte Treasure offers an unparalleled view of Thracian religious thought mirrored in art.

Another fascinating illustration is found in the burial practices preserving the visage of the Thracian horseman god - Heros. Depicted often on tombstones, Heros was a prevalent figure often found riding a galloping horse, a dog accompanying him. This regular portrayal affirmed Heros's protective role in the Thracian perception of afterlife.

Whether painted on the pottery or carved in stone and metal, these artifacts are a testament to the Thracians' deep connection to their gods, the stories they told, and the multilayered world they perceived surrounding them.

5.5. Reflection on the Thracian Belief System

The Thracians' beliefs were both mystic and pragmatic, corroborating the duality of the human experience — the mortal and the divine. Thracian mythology collectively represents not only a system of gods, stories, and rituals but also a broader cultural understanding of the world and the forces beyond. Serving as a backbone for societal order, Thracian belief systems influenced law, morality, and daily life.

In conclusion, Thracian mythology, layer upon layer, intricately woven, paints a captivating tableau of an ancient civilization's interaction with the divine and the unknown. It is a riveting narrative that continues to captivate and inspire, shedding light on the Thracians' world - an intriguing mix of reality and fantasy, human and divine, life and death.

Chapter 6. Sacred Rituals and Their Meaning

The rich tapestry of Thracian culture was heavily drenched in religious undertones. The Thracians were deeply religious people who practiced rituals and ceremonies rooted in their beliefs in various deities and the afterlife. The rituals not only represented the Thracian's profound understanding of the afterlife but also had nuances embedded in their societal norms, structures, and traditions.

6.1. The Horse Sacrifice

One of the most distinct Thracian rituals was the horse sacrifice, a solemn practice of significant socio-cultural and religious value. These were usually conducted at the death of a local noble or leader, primarily aimed at ensuring the well-being of the deceased in the afterlife. A select horse would be lavishly adorned and led to the grave or tomb of the deceased king or noble, where it would then be ritually killed. This act symbolized the unity of the ruler and his trusty steed, underlining the belief that the king would continue to ride in the idyllic pastures of the afterlife.

6.2. Funerary Rituals

Thracian funerary rites were grand spectacles where the social hierarchy was strongly emphasized. Royal burials, in particular, were opulent and meticulous affairs, with the deceased lavishly dressed and placed in a large tomb. Gold and silver, locally extracted, along with valuable ceramics and weapons were a common sight in these tombs. These treasures were meant to serve the comfort of the deceased in the afterlife and symbolize their status and prosperity during their lifetime.

The Thracian belief in life after death also extended to the treatment of the body post-death. It was often cremated, with the ashes placed in ornamental ceramic vessels called amphoras. These were then buried beneath mounds, a prominent topographical feature of Thracian landscape, each shielding a royal tomb or necropolis.

6.3. Ritual of Tattooing

The Thracians also practiced tattooing, presumably as a ritual to showcase courage or to commemorate significant life events. Inked symbols were seen as emblematic of the divine presence and protection. Detailed observations by Herodotus elucidate the Thracians' preference for tattoos, especially amongst their noble warriors. Tattoos were seen as badges of honour, symbols of warrior-brethren, their clans, and spiritual deities.

The Thracian tattooing likely incorporated indigenously symbolic motifs - Birds, horses, specific deity figures, and abstract geometric forms were popular in Thracian artifacts and probably found their way into these tattoos. The vivid imagery and symbolism represent the Thracian's spiritual connection with their gods, their cultural identity, and their socio-political order.

6.4. Feast of Dionysus

Deep in the throes of their culture and mythology were the wine rituals dedicated to Dionysus, the Thracian god of wine and ecstasy. The god was a favourite deity, embodying the fertile soils and the rich vineyards of Thrace. The Dionysian festivities usually featured ecstatic dances, music, and a lot of wine-drinking. The festive parades traversed various city-states, showcasing phallic symbols and representations of the god himself.

These wine rituals were a form of communication with the divine - an avenue seeking good health, prosperity, and fertile land. They exemplify the Thracians' deep-seated belief in nature's abundance, represented by the prolific vineyards, and their divine interaction through Dionysus. Wine, here, was the heavenly ambrosia, the sacred link between the people and their god.

6.5. Oracle Rituals

Divination or oracle rituals were another cornerstone of Thracian religious practices. Deities such as Bendis (the Thracian goddess of moon and hunt) were believed to grant visions and prophecies. They had specially designated oracle sacred sites, often on mountaintops or in dense forests where nature was the most intense. Offerings were made at these sites, followed by rituals invoking the deity. The belief that these deities would communicate through signs or visions was deeply ingrained in Thracian society.

This vivid panorama of Thracian rituals gives us an in-depth view of not just their religious convictions, but it also provides anthropological insights into the society that was. The rituals echo social hierarchies, belief systems, cultural symbolism, and inter-societal dynamics, crafting a dynamic picture of an ancient civilization that's still fertile ground for historical and anthropological exploration. The golden tale of Thracian rituals, therefore, is an intrinsic part of their cultural and historical opus.

Chapter 7. Kings and Warriors: The Pillars of Thracian Society

In the fabric of Thracian society, two figures prominently emerged as pillars of strength and direction - the mighty kings and the fearless warriors. The echoes of their vibrant history still reverberate through the ages, adding depth and dynamism to the story of these enigmatic people.

7.1. Thracian Kings: A Confluence of Power and Wisdom

Thracian kings were unique in their portrayal as physical representations of divine power. Referred frequently as 'basileus', these kings, as per ancient texts, not only played a central role in the political sphere, but also enjoyed an elevated status in religious practices.

Herodotus, a prominent Greek historian, offers a glimpse into the dual roles of a Thracian king with his description of King Sitalces. He ruled over the Odrysian kingdom of Thrace in the 5th century BC, and his reign was highlighted by military exploits and strategic treaties. Yet, he was also integral to the society's religious rituals, acting as an intermediary between the people and the divine pantheon.

The unearthing of burial sites or 'tumuli' of Thracian kings further reveal their elevated status. The Kazanlak Tomb, for instance, exhibits lavish decorations symbolizing the king's divine status, including intricate wall paintings that detail the rituals associated with the king's ascent to the afterlife.

7.2. The Warrior Code: Unleashing the Strength of the Thracians

Thracian warriors, celebrated equally for their bravery and brutality, have been immortalized by Greek and Roman historians alike. They formed the backbone of the military powerhouse that Thracian society was known for. Their tales of courage, captured in epic sagas, still resonate with awe-inspiring vigor.

Each warrior was armed with a pelta (small shield), a short sword, and often, a javelin. They were known for their aggressive strategies, rapid hit-and-run tactics, and fearless resilience in the face of the enemy. The renowned historian, Thucydides, famously stated that if the Thracians were under one ruler, they would be invincible and the strongest of all.

7.3. Warrior Women of Thrace

Among the warriors, the women held a special place. Far from passively accepting the social norms expected of the time period, Thracian women were known to have adopted the roles of warriors with unrivaled passion. They were trained in horse riding, archery, and even participated in battles.

In fact, the Thracian women warriors possibly inspired the Greek myth of the Amazons. These fierce warrior women, independent of male control, have origins traced back to the historical narrative of Thracian warrior women. It is a testament to their strength that their tales have persisted and metamorphosed into legends that symbolize female empowerment.

7.4. Kings and Warriors: The Dynamic Duo

In many ways, the Thracian kings and warriors served as the twin pillars of the society – the kings, embodying the higher ideals of divine power and political strategy, and the warriors, symbolizing the martial strength that pervaded their society.

Surviving relics from the Thracian era depict warriors paying homage to their kings, affirming the strong bond between them. One such artifact is a silver kylix from the 4th century BC, discovered at the Vassil Bojkov Collection, which depicts a warrior honoring a king. This helps to understand how these two groups interconnected and supported each other, knitting a well-structured society.

7.5. A Legacy of Valor

Today, the tales of Thracian kings and warriors, bedecked in gold and assertive in their strength, continue to fascinate historians and archaeologists alike. Their legacy set in stone and bathed in golden hues offers a vibrant peek into a society that prized power, valor, and divine favor. It stands as a potent reminder of the rich tapestry of human civilization, offering a chance for us to step back in time and understand the narratives of our ancestors.

As we conclude this exploration, we can only marvel at the extraordinary wealth of history and myth preserved in the tales of the Thracian kings and warriors. Their stories take us on a journey into a bygone era filled with mystical beliefs, fierce battles, and elaborate rituals that continue to captivate the imagination. It is a saga of a society that, in many ways, lives on in the remnants left behind, calling out to us from the depths of time.

Chapter 8. Mystery of the Thracian Tombs

Even before one starts the excursion of the Thracian tombs' exploration, it is essential to outline the historical context wrapped around these mystical structures. The Thracians, ancient inhabitants of the Southeastern European region, were a fascinating, elusive civilization that shone in splendor between 1500 BC and 300 AD. With more than two hundred tombs discovered across different periods, their funerary practices and the opulence of these tombs provides us with the most detailed tapestry of their existence and lifestyle.

8.1. The Discovery

When the first Thracian tombs were unearthed in the 19th century, they prompted waves of euphoria and fascination. Every archaeologist in Europe was stirred with the dream of discovering a myriad of gold and silver treasures confounding the layers of the Thracian graves. Aside from the vast possessions, the architectural magnificence and intricate details carved in the beautifully preserved tombs were a sight to behold.

Just off the series of discoveries came the immense Sveshtari tomb, located in northeastern Bulgaria in 1982. It was beaming with intricate carvings, and the burial chamber, encrusted with colossal stone figures, was a scene straight out of divine intervention. The tomb was finally established as a UNESCO Heritage Site in 1985, renowned for its unique architectural decor that symbolizes the fundamental structural and cultural qualities of the Thracian society.

8.2. Description of a Typical Thracian Tomb

Most Thracian tombs possess a standard architectural structure. Each tomb consists of a narrow corridor leading to a rectangular or circular burial chamber. The craftsmanship involved in creating such splendid structures is genuinely marveling considering the period of their inception. The interiors of the tombs would often feature magnificent frescoes that depicted scenes from Thracian mythology and rituals, providing us rare insights into their religious beliefs and accompanying practices.

The tomb's construction was predominantly brick and stone, with detailed engravings adorning the ceilings and walls. The significant emphasis on the Thracian tombs was noticeably on the burial chambers, they are more intricately designed often featuring impressive depictions of mythical scenes, and in cases like the Kazanlak Tomb, accompanied by richly painted murals.

8.3. Artefacts Uncovered

Apart from the architectural grandeur, the treasure trove of artefacts extracted from the Thracian tombs remains one of the most significant archaeological hauls ever unearthed. The assortment included objects of gold, silver, and bronze, in forms like jewelry, weapons, utensils, and life-sized masks. Each tomb was like a festive canvas of opulence and discernment vested with items planned for the journey to the underworld.

The Valley of Thracian Kings, as it's now commonly known, was so heavy with loot that even by today's standards, it's considered as one of the most affluent archaeological sites ever discovered. The Panagyurishte Gold Treasure unearthed from one of the tombs is a dazzling collection of gold vessels weighing around 6 kilograms, which include a phiale, an amphora, and seven rhytons.

After these many successful excavations, archaeologists have found conclusive evidence that suggests that the Thracians, much like the Ancient Egyptians, held enduring beliefs about the afterlife. Their massive burial monuments and accompanying treasures signify the ceremonial importance of death in their society.

8.4. The Enigma of the Tombs

Despite the excavations and expanded research, countless questions about the Thracian tombs are still left unanswered. Many believe the tombs were built as temples before they became resting places for the dead. Studies have not concluded whether the tombs were built by a select group of skilled artisans who traveled from town to town or if each settlement had its gifted artisans.

The specific selection of burial items and their arrangement within the tombs is another unsolved puzzle, as there doesn't seem to be a standard procedure followed in all tombs. Finally, ideas on how the Thracians managed to create such grand, architecturally sound structures without apparent usage of modern tools also remain baffling.

The examination of Thracian tombs continues even today, with archaeologists hoping to unearth more about the mysterious civilization that the Thracians were. Every new artifact, every detail spotted on an age-old fresco, brings us a step closer to understanding better this largely hushed civilization. The "Mystery of the Thracian Tombs" might be an intricate and complex puzzle, but it's one that narrates an enthralling saga of an ancient people, their beliefs, practices, craftsmanship, and their unwavering respect for death—the ultimate equalizer.

Chapter 9. Artistic Brilliance: Thracian Goldsmiths

As the dawn of civilization painted the pale colors of culture onto the canvas of human history, a collective of diverse skills came into existence. Among these realms of expertise, the Thracian goldsmiths of ancient Bulgaria began to shine with an innate brilliance that time could not fade. Positioned at the crossroads of Europe and Asia, this civilization's goldsmiths churned out awe-inspiring treasures, tales penned in gold, that render their advanced proficiency and sophistication.

9.1. The Pinnacle of Mastery

From their hands spun tales not of threads, but pure gold, sculpting monumental artifacts dripping with ornate panache. Their mastery of metal evidenced a level of sophistication that affirmed the Thracians' position at the zenith of craftsmanship.

Their ingenuity wove threads of gold into sophisticated, intricate designs. Each piece created was uniquely complex, reflecting an attention to detail that revealed their creators' knowledge of their craft and the world around them. They created masterpieces of finely detailed diadems, intricate jewelry, ceremonial masks, and decorative utensils that echoed the cultural richness and rituals of their society.

9.2. Golden Artifacts of Ancient Thracians

Countless golden artifacts, painstakingly crafted and richly ornamented, bear testimony to the sublime skill of these artisans.

One of the most emblematic discoveries, the Panagyurishte Treasure, is deemed as a benchmark of Thracian artistic expression. The magnificent trove consists of nine exquisitely designed vessels, including an amphora, three rhytons, and four fluted bowls – a testament to the Thracian civilization's zenith. Comprising over 6 kilograms of 24-carat gold, these pieces exhibit a splendid array of mythological scenes, confirming the Thracians' exceptional ability to capture narratives in metal.

Another iconic find is the golden mask of Teres, an artifact of inestimable cultural value. The mask offers a glimpse into the opulence of the Thracian nobility and their desire to transcend into the afterlife in a lavish fashion. The artist's incalculable hours, marred by painstaking precision, breathed life into this golden visage, immortalizing the Thracian king for all eternity.

9.3. Techniques of the Golden Age

The Thracian goldsmiths employed a variety of techniques, including casting, repoussé, engraving, and filigree - a testament to their unrivaled versatility.

Casting, a technique where molten gold was poured into a mould, was frequently used for larger artifacts. The moulds, often made of clay or stone, were designed with intricate detail, enabling the creation of highly complex designs.

Repoussé, a technique embodying the dexterous skill of the goldsmiths using a hammer and punch to create intricate relief work from their material's reverse side, gave life to the delicate figures on many of the discovered artifacts.

Engraving, too, featured prominently in Thracian works, allowing the artists to embellish their creations with elaborate details and motifs. With this technique, the goldsmiths were able to depict vivid scenes from mythology on items such as the rhytons from the Panagyurishte

Treasure.

Filigree represented the summit of refined intricacy. This technique, involving the twisting of thin threads of gold and soldering them onto the surface of an object, enabled the crafting of ornate designs teeming with finesse. The Thracian goldsmiths' skill in filigree was unmatched by any other known civilization at the time.

9.4. Ritualistic Affluence

The opulent, golden creations of the Thracian goldsmiths were not merely objects of decoration and status symbols; they also held significant ritualistic and religious implications.

Drinking vessels, particularly rhytons, held a special place in Thracian society. These were frequently adorned with gods and mythical creatures, symbolizing the divine favor the parties sought. Other royally owned gold items, like phialae (libation bowls), were also used in religious rituals, further exemplifying the inextricable ties between religious practices and the Thracians' gold craftsmanship.

The large amount of gold found in burial sites tells stories of a deep-rooted belief in the afterlife. The rituals involved golden masks, like that of Teres, and intricate, opulent jewelry were designed to aid the elite in their afterlife journeys, accompanying them into the world beyond.

9.5. The Legacy of the Golden Age

Preserved through millennia, the golden masterpieces left by the Thracians continue to mesmerize us and speak volumes of their highly advanced and sophisticated culture. The intricate designs, the dazzling craftsmanship, and the technical precision give us an insight into a civilization that held goldsmithing as a pinnacle of artistic expression.

In exploring the Thracian goldsmiths' work, we uncover not just artifacts, but chapters of a civilization's life, thought, and belief, illustratively narrated through the medium of gold. These golden tales continue to shed light on their creators' immense skill, hinting at a complex society where artisans were held in high regard, their hands crafting the rich history of an ancient civilization one golden artifact at a time.

As we delve deeper into these treasures' radiant depths, we don't merely discover gold; we unearth the brilliant past of the Thracians. Their legacy, solidified in gold, continues to enchant us, taking us on mesmerizing journeys back to a fantastical world of myth, fable, and legend, showcasing the brilliance of human dexterity, imagination, and expression.

Chapter 10. Influence on Neighboring Civilizations

The Thracians, being one of the earliest inhabitants of southeastern Europe, were recognized historically as tribal people. Despite lacking a centralized political organization, their indelible influence extends far beyond their territorial boundaries. Amidst the enchanting mountains and river valleys of the Balkans, the Thracians spun a rich cultural web that affected neighboring civilizations, notably the Greeks, Romans, and Byzantines. Their inimitable artistry, warfare tactics, religious practices, and societal norms played a substantial role in shaping the cultural, military, and spiritual landscapes of their more well-known neighbors.

10.1. Artistic Influence

Thracian artistic influence, especially in metalwork, reached its zenith between the 5th and 3rd century BC. Their proficiency in crafting intricate gold and silver artifacts gained the admiration of Greeks and Romans alike. Thracian art was a mix of indigenous designs coupled with the impressions of its foreign counterparts. A significant testament to this is the Rogozen Treasure. The incorporation of Thracian motifs attracted international interest and became characteristic of southwestern Eurasian artistic tradition.

Thracian styles impacted the Greek artistic scene. In fact, the Greeks owed their 'Hellenistic' art style to the influences of Thracian and other Anatolian cultures. Thracians impressed the Hellenic world with animal-shaped rhytons, fine jewelry, and especially metal vessels. The Greek adoption of Thracian armor design – notably the ceremonial 'Phrygian Helmet' – further underscores this influence.

10.2. Influence on Military

The Thracians were known for their ferocity in battle, a reputation noted in the historical writings of Herodotus and Xenophon. Their guerrilla warfare tactics strongly influenced the military strategies of neighboring civilizations. The 'falcon tactic' - a strategy where a small group of Thracians would lure enemies into a trap set by hidden forces – was prominently used by both Greek and Roman armies.

Moreover, their expertise in horse breeding provided neighboring civilizations with a unique resource that led to the procurement of superior cavalry forces. Thracian horses were deemed the best by Greek and Roman connoisseurs, and the Thracians' strategic use of cavalry was noted by neighboring civilizations. The most famous example of this is the Roman adoption of the Thracian 'Romphaia,' a broad, straight-bladed weapon advantageous in slashing through enemy infantry.

10.3. The Impact on Religion and Mythology

Thracian religious beliefs and practices had a significant influence on their neighbors, predominantly the Greeks. The uncanny similarities between Orpheus' Myth, a central figure in Greek mythology, and the Thracian God Zalmoxis, reveal the incorporation of Thracian religious figures into Greek mythology. Both are associated with the afterlife and both used rituals involving a journey to an underworld, suggesting a shared cultural nexus.

The worship of the Thracian Horseman, a divine figure usually portrayed in a hunting scene or amidst a cosmic narrative, also demonstrated heavy parallels with the Greek god of wine, Dionysus. Moreover, the Greeks borrowed Thracian Dionysian rituals, such as ecstatic dances and the use of intoxicants, suggesting a syncretism of religious practices.

10.4. Social and Political Influence

Despite the tribal nature of their society, the Thracians developed an intricate hierarchical structure that invoked admiration and influence among Greece and Rome. They were one of the first cultures to conceptualize and delineate social stratification, with clear division among aristocracy, warriors, artisans, and farmers. Their societal structure, influencing Greek polis and later Roman societal norms, indicates their pivotal role in shaping Classical Western civilization.

The Thracian political institution of 'Sanga' – a confederation of tribes under a powerful chieftain – allowed them to resist foreign occupation for centuries and shape state protocols of upcoming empires. This system is believed to have informed elements of the Roman 'Provincia' system – the management of territories outside Italy.

10.5. Conclusion

The Thracians' mark on western civilization, despite their lack of a written tradition, is both substantial and enduring. The echoes of their rich culture continue to reverberate in aspects of Western art, military strategy, religious concepts, and political ideologies. Modern understanding of Thracian culture allows us to peer into the heart of an influential civilization often overlooked in comparison to its famous neighbors. Exploring these influences reveals the undeniable power of Thracian legacy and the potent strands they've woven into the cultural tapestry of Europe.

Chapter 11. Legacy of the Thracians: A Retrospective Glance

The Thracian civilization emerged in southeastern Europe, inhabiting portions of modern-day Turkey, Greece, and Bulgaria. With roots stretching back to 3000 BC, this culturally complex and technologically sophisticated society is still mostly shrouded in mystery, yet its influence upon the broader European society is indubitable.

11.1. The Origins of the Thracian Civilization

Thracians were not a singular, homogeneous entity; instead, they were composed of numerous separate tribes, each with its distinctive characteristics. While their earliest roots lie in the Bronze Age, they emerged as a separate entity by the 1st millennium BC. Their unwillingness to unite politically rendered them vulnerable to foreign invaders, yet it is remarkable how significantly their cultural influence permeated the ancient world despite this.

Notable for their exquisite metalwork and formidable warriors, the Thracians left a substantial mark on ancient Greek and Roman culture. Skilled artisans, resilient warriors, and seafarers, their legacy is as expansive as their territories once were.

11.2. The Emanation of Thracian Art and Metalwork

One of the Thracian civilization's most profound inheritances is their exceptional skill in metalwork, primarily gold and silver. Artisans crafted intricate designs into weapons, jewelry, and religious artifacts. Often depicting scenes from mythology or significant battles, these items served as status symbols for the Thracian elite.

Many of these pieces have been preserved, providing a glimpse into the socio-cultural fabric of ancient Thracian society. They unveil an image of Thracian society starkly punctuated by warfare, religion, and a deep-rooted sense of artistry and aesthetics.

11.3. Warriors of Thracia

The Thracians were a warrior culture. Their fame across the ancient world stemmed from their unyielding nature and martial prowess. The Greeks chronicled tales of their boldness and resilience. They even integrated Thracians into their legends, immortalizing Thracian warriors like Orpheus and Spartacus.

The warrior class held high social status. Thracian weaponry and armor were renowned and significantly influenced the ways Greeks and Romans equipped their forces. They served as mercenaries, auxiliares, and gladiators, their courage and hardiness making them indispensable assets on the battlefield.

11.4. Interfaces of Influence: Greek, Persian, and Roman

Throughout history, the Thracians came into frequent contact with Greeks, Persians, and Romans, substantially influencing, and being influenced by these cultures.

In terms of religion, the Thracians shared many similarities with the Greeks. They believed in the afterlife and worshipped a pantheon of gods and goddesses. Their belief system was heavily influenced by their Greek neighbors, with observers noting similarities in burial practices and adornments.

The Persian influence on Thracians is seen in their lifestyle, arts, and military strategy. The glimpse of Thracian society from historical texts and archeology points to a mixture of indigenous elements and Iranian influences, particularly during the Achaemenid period.

One cannot miss the Roman footprint on Thracian society when studying the late Thracian civilization. After Rome comprehensively defeated the Thracians, many facets of Roman society, including architecture, urban planning, and administrative systems, began to emerge in Thracian society. In return, Thracian cultural aspects, notably their religious beliefs and artistry, blended into Roman legacy.

11.5. Linguistic Legacy

Lost in the sands of time, the Thracian language adds to the enigma of this civilization. Notwithstanding shared elements with Hellenic languages, Thracian remains categorized as a separate Indo-European language. Its corpus is restricted to a small array of names, place names, and a few phrases found in Greek and Roman texts. While our knowledge remains limited, this uniquely Thracian language underscores the distinctiveness of the Thracian identity in the ancient world.

11.6. Conclusion: The Echoes of Thracian Legacy

The Thracian civilization, albeit less familiar to most, has undeniably shaped the trajectory of Europe's early history. The ancient Greeks and Romans, powerful shapers of the world as we know it, borrowed, exchanged, and adopted aspects of Thracian culture, be it their martial prowess, artistic inclinations, spiritual beliefs or social constructs.

Despite their fragmentation, the Thracians manifested rich cultural, artistic, and martial traditions that remarkably contrasted their socio-political division. Today, the recovered Thracian artefacts continue to mesmerize us with their ornate beauty and intricate design, allowing us a semi-transparent glance into the vibrant tapestry of the Thracian world. Ultimately, the legacy of the Thracians serves as cobblestones to Europe's formative path, underpinning the cultural evolution of many present-day practices.

Printed in Great Britain
by Amazon